THE
NBA
A HISTORY OF HOOPS

Published by Creative Education
P.O. Box 227, Mankato, Minnesota 56002
Creative Education is an imprint of The Creative Company
www.thecreativecompany.us

Design and production by Christine Vanderbeek
Art direction by Rita Marshall

Printed by Corporate Graphics in the United States of America

Photographs by Dreamstime (Munktcu), Getty Images (Bill Baptist/NBAE,
Andrew D. Bernstein/NBAE, Nathaniel S. Butler/NBAE, Andy Caulfield, Jim
Cummins/NBAE, James Drake/Sports Illustrated, Noah Graham/NBAE, Mark
Green, John W. McDonough/Sports Illustrated, Fernando Medina/NBAE, Dick
Raphael/NBAE, SM/AIUEO), iStockphoto (Brandon Laufenberg)

Library of Congress Cataloging-in-Publication Data
Frisch, Nate.
The story of the Houston Rockets / by Nate Frisch.
p. cm. — (The NBA: a history of hoops)
Includes index.
Summary: The history of the Houston Rockets professional basketball
team from its start in San Diego, California, in 1967 to today,
spotlighting the franchise's greatest players and moments.
ISBN 978-1-58341-945-8
1. Houston Rockets (Basketball team)—History—Juvenile literature. I. Title.
GV885.52.H68F7557 2010   796.323'64097641411—dc22   2009035026

CPSIA: 120109 PO1093

First Edition
2 4 6 8 9 7 5 3 1

Page 3: Forward Luis Scola
Pages 4–5: Forward Tracy McGrady

THE STORY OF THE

HOUSTON ROCKETS

NATE FRISCH

CREATIVE EDUCATION

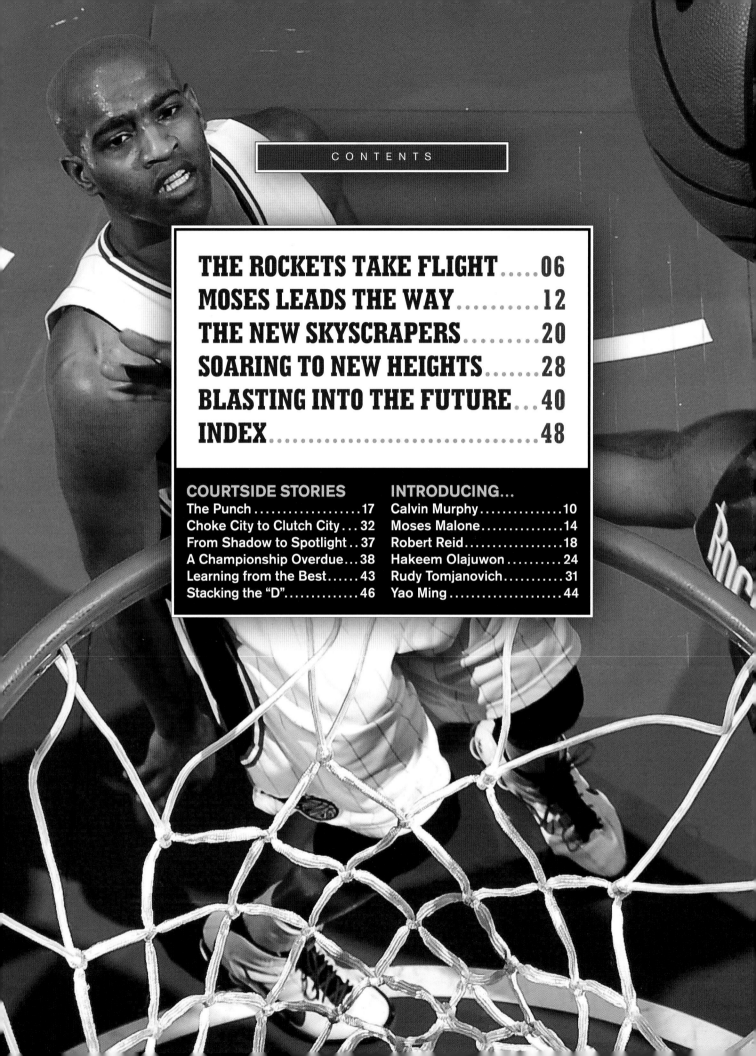

CONTENTS

CHAPTER ONE

THE ROCKETS TAKE FLIGHT

Houston, Texas, is a city that embraces the old and the new. The city was named in 1836 after General Sam Houston, who led the army that won Texas's independence from Mexico. From a utilitarian settlement that once revolved around the cotton and oil industries, Houston grew into the fourth-largest city in America and a focal point of modern technology. Impressive skyscrapers now form the heart of the city, and Houston is home to the Johnson Space Center—the headquarters for America's astronaut training program.

A National Basketball Association (NBA) team named the Rockets seemed natural for a city with a National Aeronautics and Space Administration (NASA) space center. However, the well-matched named was mostly a coincidence. The franchise actually got its start in San Diego, California. It had been named the Rockets in reference to that city's theme of "A City in Motion," and the fact that NASA rockets were manufactured there. When the team relocated to Houston in 1971, the name remained, and the Rockets have been aiming for the stars ever since.

Rockets built for America's space program factor prominently into the industrial history of both cities that have hosted the Rockets franchise.

dded to the NBA as an expansion team in 1967, the San Diego Rockets struggled to launch. The franchise's first draft pick was guard Pat Riley. Riley ultimately had a great career as an NBA coach, but as a player, he couldn't prevent the Rockets from finishing with a league-worst 15–67 record. The only upside to the lousy record was that it gave San Diego the top overall pick in the 1968 NBA Draft.

The Rockets used that pick to draft forward/center Elvin Hayes. The 6-foot-9 Hayes, known to fans as "The Big E," had a sensational rookie season, tallying 28.4 points and 17.1 boards per game. He boasted a turnaround jump shot that was virtually unstoppable, and he attacked the glass like a wild man. "Rebounding is a rough proposition," he once noted. "But it's one of the ways I make my living, so it's something I force myself to tolerate, no matter how many bruises I wind up with."

Although his initial stay with the Rockets would last just four seasons, Hayes was the franchise's first true star and the first of what would become a long line of dominating post players. He led the Rockets to their first playoff appearance after the 1968–69 season, but the team regressed the following year.

To become a legitimate threat, the Rockets needed a more balanced roster. In 1970, they drafted forward Rudy Tomjanovich and guard Calvin Murphy. The 6-foot-8 Tomjanovich offered a soft shooting touch, a knack for working the offensive boards, and a steadying presence on the court. The 5-foot-9 Murphy, meanwhile, brought lightning quickness to both ends of the court, and his accurate, high-arcing jump shots proved difficult for even the tallest opponents to defend.

Elvin Hayes kicked off his NBA career by scoring 54 points in one game during his rookie season—a total that remained a career best.

SIMPLY PUT, CALVIN MURPHY WAS SMALL. His early ambitions were also small. Looking back on his career, Murphy recalled, "My only dream was that I wanted to start for my high school basketball team, the Norwalk High School Bears." Ultimately, Murphy made up for his short stature with big talent. Although he was usually the smallest player on the court in any game, Murphy was also one of the quickest. This quickness made him a sticky defender and a shifty scorer. Murphy also had a high-arcing shot that drove would-be shot blockers crazy as it soared over them with pinpoint accuracy. When Murphy didn't have his view obstructed by taller players, he made the most of it. The point guard set NBA records for consecutive free throws made (78) and free throw percentage (.958) during the 1980–81 season. The long-time Rockets standout also represented stable leadership for the franchise. Murphy was inducted into the Basketball Hall of Fame in 1993. Afterward, one of his former high school coaches joked, "Yeah, I reckon he was good enough to make our team."

INTRODUCING...

CALVIN MURPHY

POSITION GUARD
HEIGHT 5-FOOT-9
ROCKETS SEASONS 1970–83

ed by Hayes, Murphy, and Tomjanovich, the Rockets improved to 40–
42 in 1970–71. However, low fan attendance prompted the team's
owners to move the franchise to Houston in 1971. After the club's
record worsened in the 1971–72 campaign, the Rockets traded Hayes to
the Baltimore Bullets for versatile swingman Jack Marin.

Hayes's departure put a dent in the Rockets' metal, but improving
performance from Tomjanovich and Murphy kept the team competi-
tive, and in 1974–75, the duo lead the Rockets to their first playoff
berth since relocating to Houston. In the first round of the postseason,
Houston shocked the favored New York Knicks in a three-game series.
However, the Rockets were then outclassed in the second round by a
talented Boston Celtics team.

CHAPTER TWO

MOSES LEADS THE WAY

To move up another rung on the NBA ladder, the Rockets put their hopes in center Moses Malone. Malone had professional experience in the American Basketball Association (ABA), and the Rockets became his second NBA team (after he played a mere two games for the Buffalo Braves) when he joined them via trade during the 1976–77 season. A bruising player, "Mo" Malone gave Houston the potent scorer and rebounder it had been lacking since Hayes's departure. Also new to Houston that season was rookie guard John Lucas, who provided confident ball handling and stability. "John doesn't overwhelm you with talent," said Rockets guard Mike Newlin. "He's just smooth. He asserts himself without infringing on anyone else's space, which is really an art."

This bolstered lineup earned the franchise's first winning record at 49–33. After a first-round bye in the playoffs, Houston surged past the Bullets, who were led by former

Although never a star, guard Mike Newlin added steady scoring and scrappy play to the Rockets' lineup throughout the 1970s.

ALTHOUGH A POWERFUL AND SKILLED PLAYER, EVEN MOSES MALONE SOMETIMES FOUND HIMSELF IN SITUATIONS WHERE GETTING AN OPEN SHOT WAS DIFFICULT. However, just when defenders thought they had forced "Mo" into an ugly shot, the ball would carom off the backboard right back at him—just as he'd planned. With the ball returned to him and the defender out of position, Malone would score a quick put-back before the opposition could even react. As NBA coach Bill Fitch once noted, "[Malone] starts to rebound just before he shoots." It was this kind of ingenuity and workhorse effort that made Malone one of the greatest rebounders in NBA history. He once pulled in 37 boards in a single game and set NBA records for most offensive rebounds in a game (21) as well as in a season (587). Still, Malone was about more than just sweat and muscle. He kept scorekeepers busy and was a well-rounded defender, too. Mo earned two NBA Most Valuable Player (MVP) awards while playing for the Rockets and led the team to its first NBA Finals appearance in 1981.

INTRODUCING...

MOSES MALONE

POSITION CENTER
HEIGHT 6-FOOT-10
ROCKETS SEASONS 1976–82

Rockets star Elvin Hayes. In the Eastern Conference finals, the Rockets

played six tough games against the Philadelphia 76ers. However, at the

end of a tight Game 6, a controversial charging call against Lucas ended

Houston's hopes of an NBA Finals appearance.

The Rockets seemed poised to go a step farther the next year before

a frightening incident derailed them. During a midseason game

against the Los Angeles Lakers, a fight broke out, and hulking

Lakers forward Kermit Washington hit Tomjanovich in the face with a

devastating punch that ended his season. Without Tomjanovich's scoring

and leadership, Houston finished 28–54.

In 1978–79, Tomjanovich was back, and Malone enjoyed perhaps his

finest season. The hardworking center averaged 24.8 points and 17.6

rebounds a game to earn the NBA MVP award. Unfortunately, Houston

fell to the Atlanta Hawks in the first round of the playoffs. The Rockets

fared only marginally better in the next postseason, reaching the second

round before being swept by the Celtics.

The Rockets went a mediocre 40–42 in 1980–81 but sneaked into

the playoffs. Once there, they stunned the league by defeating three

favored opponents to reach the NBA Finals. Few fans or experts gave

Houston any chance against star forward Larry Bird and the Celtics, but

the Rockets—behind Malone, Murphy, and swingman Robert Reid—won two games before their unlikely run was ended in Game 6. "Every member of our team can take great pride in playing on a team that people said wouldn't win a single playoff game," said Houston coach Del Harris.

Over the next couple of years, many of Houston's familiar faces disappeared. Tomjanovich retired before the 1981–82 season, and Murphy's playing time dropped. Despite another MVP season from Malone, the Rockets were bounced from the playoffs in round one. Afterward, Houston decided it could not afford to keep its star center, and Malone was traded to the 76ers for mediocre center Caldwell Jones and a future draft pick. This left a gaping hole in the Houston frontcourt, and in 1982–83, the Rockets fell to an embarrassing 14–68. It seemed the Rockets had run out of fuel.

COURTSIDE STORIES

THE PUNCH

Rudy Tomjanovich in a protective mask during a 1979 game.

COMING OFF A STRONG PLAYOFF SEASON, HOPES WERE HIGH AMONG THE HOUSTON FAITHFUL FOR THE 1977-78 SEASON. On December 9, 1977, those hopes were shattered. That night, an ugly on-court fight broke out between players from the Lakers and the Rockets. It began with an altercation between Lakers center Kareem Abdul-Jabbar and Houston center Kevin Kunnert. Rockets forward Rudy Tomjanovich rushed into the melee trying to act as peacemaker when powerful 6-foot-8 Lakers forward Kermit Washington hit him with a heavy right cross. The punch was so brutal that it shattered Tomjanovich's face, nearly killing him. Although his face needed extensive reconstructive surgery and five months to heal, Tomjanovich made a remarkable return to the court the following year, averaging 19 points and 7.7 rebounds per game. Washington, who was suspended for two months by the NBA for the incident, still has trouble living down "The Punch." "Rudy realizes that I'm sorry, and I'm glad that he's forgiven me," Washington said years later. "Maybe when I die, they won't have on my grave, 'The guy who hit Rudy Tomjanovich.'"

ROBERT REID

POSITION GUARD / FORWARD
HEIGHT 6-FOOT-8
ROCKETS SEASONS 1977–82, 1983–88

ROBERT REID'S STATS WEREN'T ALWAYS OVER-WHELMING, BUT NUMBERS DIDN'T TELL HIS WHOLE STORY. A dogged defender, Reid was often charged with covering the opposing team's top scorer. In Houston's surprising 1981 playoff run, Reid averaged more than one block and two steals per game while defending star players such as guard Magic Johnson and forward Larry Bird. After taking the 1982–83 season off to focus on religious ministry, Reid returned to provide leadership and stability to a young Houston roster. Late in the 1985–86 season, an injury left the Rockets without a point guard. Reid shifted from backup guard/forward to starting point guard and proceeded to guide the Rockets all the way to the NBA Finals. Throughout his successes, Reid remained humble. Following a game in which he tallied 19 points and 10 offensive rebounds while holding Larry Bird to 8 points, reporters wondered if there was some secret to the performance. Reid told them, "I got up this morning, ate some Fruit Loops, watched Tarzan save Boy from an alligator on television, and came down here to take my warm-ups."

CHAPTER THREE

THE NEW SKYSCRAPERS

The silver lining to Houston's woeful record was that it gave the team the first overall pick in the 1983 NBA Draft. The Rockets used the selection to take center Ralph Sampson, a three-time College Player of the Year from the University of Virginia. The team also landed talented forward Rodney McCray with the third overall pick.

The 7-foot-4 Sampson averaged 21 points, 11.1 rebounds, and 2.4 blocks per game in 1983–84 to earn Rookie of the Year honors. Along with McCray, he boosted the Rockets to 29–53—a significant improvement, but still among the NBA's worst records. The Rockets won a coin toss to secure the first choice in the 1984 Draft, and with it, they selected another seven-footer—this time choosing center Akeem (later Hakeem) "The Dream" Olajuwon.

The imposing frontcourt duo of Olajuwon and Sampson, quickly nicknamed the "Twin Towers," not only posted impressive scoring and rebounding numbers but chased opposing offenses out of the paint with their shot-blocking prowess. Many observers thought the Rockets were crazy in

The "Twin Towers" of Ralph Sampson and Akeem Olajuwon ruled the lane defensively in 1984–85, blocking a combined 388 shots.

stockpiling two great players who played the same position, putting a combined 14 feet, 4 inches of center on the court each night. Houston coach Bill Fitch disagreed. "I don't know a coach who would tell you that Olajuwon and Sampson can't play together in the same lineup," Fitch said. "Then again, we could cut them in half and make four guards."

In 1985–86, Sampson and Olajuwon, backed by McCray, Lucas, and efficient guard Lewis Lloyd, soared to a 51–31 mark and blasted into the playoffs. In the Western Conference finals, Houston had the mighty Lakers on the ropes, leading the series three games to one. In Game 5, with the score tied 112–112 and one second on the clock, McCray hurled an inbound pass from mid-court. Sampson leaped to catch the pass and, still hanging in the air, lobbed the ball toward the basket 12 feet away. The shot arced over Lakers center Kareem Abdul-Jabbar, bounced high off the rim, and rattled in to clinch the Rockets' spot in the NBA Finals. Unfortunately, the Celtics—who reigned as a powerhouse throughout the '80s— then thwarted the Rockets once again, claiming the trophy in six games.

The Rockets experienced a letdown the following year and broke up

the Twin Towers in 1987, trading Sampson away and turning to Olajuwon to lead the team. The still-improving Olajuwon boasted amazing agility and devastating moves in the low post. He attributed much of his crafty footwork to his experience playing soccer, which had been his favorite sport while growing up in Nigeria. "Olajuwon is blessed with grace, ability, and quickness…," marveled former Rockets guard Rick Barry. "His edge is his ability to outdo his opponents physically: outjump, outquick, outrun them."

Starting with the 1987–88 campaign, the Rockets enjoyed four straight playoff seasons, adding muscular power forward Otis Thorpe and quick guards Kenny Smith and Vernon Maxwell along the way. Unfortunately, each postseason ended quickly, as Houston suffered first-round defeats every time.

A HUMBLE AND GENTLE MAN OFF THE COURT, HAKEEM "THE DREAM" OLAJUWON WAS A NIGHT-MARE FOR OPPOSING TEAMS ON THE HARDWOOD. Although the Nigerian center had never played organized basketball until he was a high school senior, he was soon routinely swatting shots on one end of the court, then dazzling fans and frustrating defenders with his agile moves and deft shooting touch on the other end. Olajuwon developed a set of offensive fakes and spins that was so difficult to defend it was given its own name—the Dream Shake. The Dream Shake was unpredictable and nearly indefensible, capped off by a variety of lay-ins, fadeaways, or hook shots. Fellow NBA center Shaquille O'Neal calculated, "Hakeem has five moves, then four countermoves. That gives him 20 moves."

The pinnacle of Olajuwon's career came in 1993–94, when he led the Rockets to an NBA championship and was named both NBA MVP and Defensive Player of the Year. When he retired in 2002, Olajuwon was the only player in NBA history to rank in the top 10 in career scoring, rebounding, blocked shots, and steals.

In the midst of an unremarkable 1991–92 season, former Rockets star Rudy Tomjanovich took over as interim head coach. Houston hoped that the steady leadership he had provided on the court as a player would carry over to the bench. The Rockets failed to reach the playoffs, but Tomjanovich proved himself capable enough to be named full-time head coach after the season.

In 1992-93, Olajuwon excelled under Tomjanovich, posting his best statistical season yet. Rookie forward Robert Horry—a rangy defender with an accurate shooting touch—added versatility and immediately cracked the starting lineup. Following a strong regular season that featured 55 victories, Houston won its first postseason series in 6 years. The Rockets' second-round matchup with the Seattle SuperSonics was an evenly waged battle that culminated in an overtime period in Game 7. The Rockets were edged out, 103–100, but they aspired to go higher yet. "It's tough losing close ones," said Horry, "but it shows how close we are."

Robert Horry did a little bit of everything for Houston in the early '90s, including setting teammates up for scores with slick passes.

CHAPTER FOUR

SOARING TO NEW HEIGHTS

In 1993, after winning three straight NBA titles with the Chicago Bulls, superstar guard Michael Jordan took a break from basketball, temporarily ending Chicago's era of domination. The top teams across the league were eager to claim the now vulnerable championship trophy. The timing worked out perfectly for the Rockets. Tomjanovich's starting five remained intact from the previous season, and Olajuwon was at the peak of his career. In 1993–94, he averaged 27.3 points, 11.9 boards, and 3.7 blocks per game, earning both the league MVP and Defensive Player of the Year awards. Thanks to his dominance, Houston flew out of the gate, winning its first 15 games and eventually winning both the Midwest Division and the second seed in the Western Conference playoffs.

In the postseason, the Rockets navigated a gauntlet of talented and experienced opponents—the Portland Trail Blazers, Phoenix Suns, and Utah Jazz—to reach the NBA Finals. There they faced the New York Knicks—a team much like their own. The rugged and confident Knicks were led by center Patrick Ewing, whose stats and accolades rivaled Olajuwon's. And like Olajuwon, Ewing had a supporting cast of big forwards and aggressive guards.

Brawny forward Otis Thorpe quietly assembled an outstanding NBA career, averaging 14 points and 8.2 boards per game across 17 seasons.

The Finals proved to be a hard-fought series. Down three games to two, the Rockets held on to win Game 6 by a score of 86–84 when Olajuwon blocked a potential game-winning three-pointer by Knicks guard John Starks. Game 7 was played at Houston's arena, The Summit. In a game in which the usual stars struggled to make shots, Houston's guard trio of Maxwell, Smith, and rookie Sam Cassell combined to hit 14 of 24 field-goal attempts and 13 of 14 free throws. Their efficient contributions helped Houston claim a 90–84 victory and the franchise's first NBA title. "This was a tough battle," said a jubilant Olajuwon. "It was truly a championship game. If you write a book, you can't write it any better."

After waiting 26 years for their first NBA crown, the Rockets were poised to defend it the next season, but their Western Conference opponents were growing ever stronger. Rather than wait for the competition to catch up, the Rockets aimed to stay ahead of the curve. Midway through the season, Houston traded Thorpe to Portland for All-Star guard Clyde "The Glide" Drexler. Even so, the conference had become so daunting that the Rockets earned only the sixth-best record.

RUDY TOMJANOVICH WAS ONE OF THE ROCKETS' FIRST STARS. His most noticeable skill was his accurate shooting, as he knocked down more than 50 percent of his shots during his career. "Rudy T" also was a smart ball handler and could be a tough rebounder. This versatility earned him five All-Star Game selections. Tomjanovich had a great understanding of the game and a willingness to do whatever was needed—characteristics that translated well to his coaching career. But he was actually reluctant to become a head coach. "I really loved being an assistant coach," he said. "I didn't want the spotlight." Once he took up that post, though, Tomjanovich worked hard and was well-liked by his players. He could be seen and heard pacing the sidelines, hoarsely shouting instructions to players and arguing with refs. Yet for all his intensity during games, he was modest off the court, accepting blame for the team's failures while giving players the credit for successes. But there was often enough credit to go around. In just his second and third full seasons as head coach, Tomjanovich guided the Rockets to back-to-back NBA championships.

INTRODUCING...

RUDY TOMJANOVICH

POSITION FORWARD, COACH
HEIGHT 6-FOOT-8
ROCKETS SEASONS
AS PLAYER 1970–81
AS COACH 1992–2003

CHOKE CITY TO CLUTCH CITY

The Rockets do battle with the Suns in the 1994 playoffs.

"CHOKE CITY." THIS WAS THE NEW NICKNAME FOR HOUSTON SUGGESTED IN A NEWSPAPER HEADLINE FOLLOWING THE ROCKETS' BACK-TO-BACK COLLAPSES IN ROUND TWO OF THE 1994 PLAYOFFS. In Game 1 against the Phoenix Suns, Houston let an 18-point lead slip away. They did one better (or worse) in Game 2, wasting a 20-point lead in the fourth quarter. Both losses were on the Rockets' home court, and hopes were rapidly fading. "We traveled directly to Phoenix after the game," center Hakeem Olajuwon said. "That was a terrible flight. It was silent on the plane, as if somebody had died. Nobody was prepared for what had happened."

In Game 3, the Rockets were trailing by nine at halftime. However, it was Houston's turn for a comeback, and the Rockets crushed the Suns in the second half. Another step-up performance then clinched Game 4 for Houston. Having evened the series in Phoenix, the Rockets returned home to a city with a new nickname: "Clutch City." The Rockets cemented that label by not only winning the Phoenix series but by going on to victory in the NBA Finals as well.

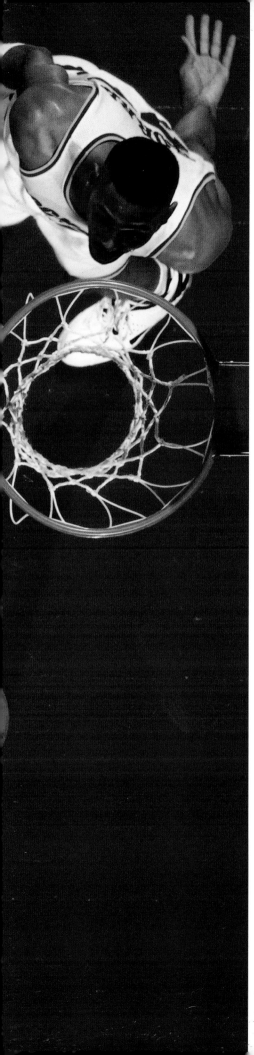

nce the postseason began, Houston showed its mettle. Olajuwon and Drexler consistently gave impressive performances, but even so, the Rockets would have been grounded had it not been for clutch shots by Horry, Smith, Cassell, and guard Mario Elie. Houston's team efforts spurred it past the West's top three teams to return to the NBA Finals. In the Finals, the Rockets took on the Orlando Magic, who featured enormous center Shaquille O'Neal and swift guard Penny Hardaway. Although possibly the league's most exciting young team, Orlando was outclassed and outplayed by the more experienced Rockets, and Houston swept the series to repeat as champions. Afterward, Tomjanovich said, "We had nonbelievers all along the way, and I have one thing to say to those nonbelievers: Don't ever underestimate the heart of a champion."

Pages 34–35: Clyde Drexler displays his trademark glide.

After falling short in the 1996 playoffs, the Rockets traded away four players for burly forward Charles Barkley, giving Houston's lineup three future Hall-of-Famers. Barkley helped the 1996–97 Rockets go 57–25 and push as far as the Western Conference finals, but Utah thwarted a return to the championship series. Injuries led to a mediocre season the next year, and Drexler retired. To fill the void, Houston traded for another veteran superstar—Chicago forward Scottie Pippen. The Rockets put together a solid regular season but lost in the first round of the 1999 playoffs. Afterward, Pippen was traded to the Trail Blazers for six players, including center Kelvin Cato and forward Walt Williams.

In the 1999–2000 season, a knee injury ended Barkley's career, and age and injuries decreased Olajuwon's effectiveness. Without these perennial All-Stars leading the way, the Rockets' impressive run came to an end, and they missed the playoffs for the first time in eight years.

FROM SHADOW TO SPOTLIGHT

Mario Elie knocks down a "three."

ONE OF THE MOST FAMOUS SHOTS IN ROCKETS HISTORY CAME FROM AN UNEXPECTED SOURCE. In the second round of the 1995 playoffs, Houston was down three games to one versus Phoenix and on the verge of elimination. Some members of that Suns team were still bitter about Houston's round-two series comeback the previous year and publicly promised it wouldn't happen again. Despite such guarantees, the Rockets evened the series by winning Games 5 and 6. Then, in Game 7, the Rockets and Suns were tied in the closing moments, and Houston guard Mario Elie had the ball. The journeyman Elie had played for four teams in his six NBA seasons, typically coming off the bench. Everyone in Phoenix's America West Arena expected him to pass the ball to star center Hakeem Olajuwon. "Dream was wide-open, but I had my feet set," Elie said. "I let it go, and it felt good." The three-pointer rained through the net with 7.1 seconds remaining, Elie blew the Suns' bench a goodbye kiss, and the Rockets won 115–114 and went on to capture the NBA title.

Hakeem Olajuwon (left) fights for the ball during the 1995 playoffs.

A CHAMPIONSHIP OVERDUE

FOR TWO YEARS STRAIGHT IN THE EARLY 1980S, THE UNIVERSITY OF HOUSTON COUGARS LOST IN COLLEGE BASKETBALL'S NATIONAL CHAMPIONSHIP GAME. That highfly-ing, dunk-happy squad—affectionately known as "Phi Slamma Jamma"—included center Akeem "The Dream" Olajuwon and guard Clyde "The Glide" Drexler. In the NBA, both play-ers quickly emerged as stars, though championships still eluded them. With their respective NBA teams—Olajuwon in Houston and Drexler in Portland—each player experienced runner-up seasons like they had in college, being bested in the NBA Finals by the likes of the Boston Celtics, Detroit Pistons, and Chicago Bulls. Then Olajuwon's Rockets won the 1994 NBA champion-ship, and late in the 1994–95 season, Houston traded with the Trail Blazers to bring Drexler back "home." The duo of Olajuwon and Drexler powered the Rockets through the playoffs and to a four-game sweep of the Magic in the 1995 Finals to at last give the reunited teammates a championship season to-gether. "It was great to win the champi-onship in the place where it all began," said Drexler.

CHAPTER FIVE

BLASTING INTO THE FUTURE

The Rockets had grown accustomed to leadership from star veterans and to running their offense through the low post. But by the year 2000, a young, enthusiastic backcourt was emerging as Houston's focal point. Explosive point guard Steve Francis and rapid-fire shooting guard Cuttino Mobley proved a difficult duo for opponents to handle. Unfortunately, while Francis and Mobley were lighting up scoreboards, the Rockets ranked last in the NBA in defense by the end of the 2001–02 campaign and finished with a 28–54 record.

The Rockets' struggles helped them obtain the top overall pick in the 2002 NBA Draft. Hoping to bring back the days of a dominating post presence, Houston used the selection to draft 7-foot-6 center Yao Ming from Shanghai, China. Yao improved the team's defense and added an inside threat to an otherwise perimeter-oriented offense, boosting the Rockets back over the .500 mark. His first-year numbers weren't staggering, but the young giant showed great potential. "It will take time to adapt," said Yao on learning the NBA game, "but I think I can handle it."

Cuttino Mobley was a cornerstone of the Rockets' rebuilding efforts in the early 2000s, leading the team in scoring in 2001–02.

Playing under new coach Jeff Van Gundy in the new Toyota Center, Yao and the Rockets further improved the next season, reaching the playoffs after a four-year drought. Then, in 2004, Francis and Mobley were traded to Orlando for forward Tracy McGrady. "T-Mac" had led the league in scoring the previous season and teamed up nicely with Yao to give the Rockets a potent one-two punch. Not just a scorer, the 6-foot-8 McGrady ranked either first or second on the team in assists, rebounds, and steals in 2004–05. Behind this effort, the Rockets won 51 games and took the Dallas Mavericks to 7 games in the opening round of the playoffs. Although it was crushed in Game 7, 116–76, Houston remained confident in its future prospects. "It was really not befitting how we played and conducted ourselves this year," said Van Gundy following the blowout loss. "The way it ended does not reflect well on myself or the team, but it does not affect my overall pride."

Injuries plagued the Rockets in 2005–06, and as Yao and McGrady missed a combined 60 games, the Rockets sputtered. The two stars were hurt much of the following season as well, but usually one or the other was able to suit up each game, and that was often enough to keep Houston formidable. Each player averaged about 25 points per game when healthy, and the Rockets posted a solid 52–30 record. Unfortunately, they then suffered another disappointing Game 7 loss (this time to Utah) in a first-round playoff clash.

WHEN THE ROCKETS ACQUIRED ROOKIE CENTER YAO MING IN 2002, HE WAS ALREADY A TALENTED PLAYER. Still, he was only 22 years old, and the Rockets saw potential for tremendous growth. After Yao's first season, the Rockets brought in Patrick Ewing as an assistant coach. Ewing had assembled a Hall of Fame career playing center for New York. In fact, it was Ewing and his Knicks whom the Rockets had narrowly defeated in the 1994 NBA Finals. Houston was eager to have him contribute to the development of young Yao. The following year, Houston added veteran Dikembe Mutombo to the roster. "Mount Mutombo" was among the greatest defensive centers of all time. He also demonstrated great leadership, work habits, and personal dignity, making him an ideal role model for the maturing Yao. If that wasn't enough, Yao began training with Rockets legend Hakeem Olajuwon, practicing spin moves, drop steps, and jump hooks. Referring to Yao's tutelage under three historic centers, one team official noted, "If he picks up even a fraction of what these guys can teach, the NBA had better watch out."

INTRODUCING...

YAO MING

POSITION CENTER
HEIGHT 7-FOOT-6
ROCKETS SEASONS 2002–PRESENT

WHEN THE ROCKETS SELECTED YAO MING FROM CHINA WITH THE FIRST PICK IN THE 2002 NBA DRAFT, THEY ACQUIRED A GIANT. Even among other NBA centers, Yao was often a half foot taller and 50 pounds heavier than anyone else on the court. He performed the tasks expected of such a big man—challenging opponents' shots and hauling in rebounds—but it was his polished offensive ability that separated Yao from other seven-foot-plus centers. For such a huge man, Yao developed impressive footwork and body control, allowing him to get good position under the basket and keep defenders off balance. An accurate shooter, he consistently made more than 50 percent of his shots from the floor and better than 80 percent of his free throws. Basketball skills aside, Yao had a positive and caring outlook on life, as coach Rudy Tomjanovich quickly noticed. "He has leadership qualities, and he's a guy that sets a fantastic image and example for people," Tomjanovich said. "I think when you find a player that has talent and that type of personality, the combination is truly something."

IN HAKEEM OLAJUWON, HOUSTON BOASTED ONE OF THE GREATEST DEFENSIVE PLAYERS IN NBA HISTORY. However, in 2001–02, a year after his departure, the Rockets' defense plummeted to last in the league rankings. The addition of center Yao Ming helped the following year, and forward Tracy McGrady added more defensive competence a couple years later. However, the Rockets seemed determined to take defense to the extreme and over the next few years added center Dikembe Mutombo and forwards Shane Battier and Ron Artest. Collectively, the trio had been named to the NBA's All-Defensive team 10 times and had earned a combined 5 Defensive Player of the Year awards. Although Mutombo was near the end of his career, his size (7-foot-2) and timing for swatting shots remained constant. The long-limbed Battier and stout Artest, meanwhile, could pin down a wide range of opponents. Said Battier of Artest, "He's the only guy I've ever seen who's able to guard [point guard] Aaron Brooks and then turn around two minutes later and guard Yao Ming." It surprised no one that Houston's defense was soon again ranked among the league's stingiest.

COURTSIDE STORIES

STACKING THE "D"

Shane Battier applies pressure to Lakers star Kobe Bryant.

I n 2007–08, Yao and McGrady were again limited by nagging injuries. But under new head coach Rick Adelman, a supporting cast that included shifty point guard Rafer Alston, savvy forward Shane Battier, and rookie forwards Luis Scola and Carl Landry picked up the slack. The Rockets won 55 games, but they quickly lost to Utah in the playoffs for the second straight year. Despite Houston's string of first-round failures, the Rockets believed they were on course. "[We've got] a bunch of young guys that have a bright future," McGrady said.

McGrady missed more than half the 2008–09 season with a knee injury, but the addition of gritty forward Ron Artest and the development of Scola and speedy second-year point guard Aaron Brooks helped the Rockets finish 53–29 and make it over the first-round playoff hump by beating the Trail Blazers. Unfortunately, the 2009–10 season represented a step back. Artest left town to join the Lakers, Yao missed the entire year after having foot surgery, and after the injury-prone McGrady was traded to New York in a swap that brought high-scoring guard Kevin Martin to town, the Rockets finished just 42–40.

Like the city of Houston, the Rockets have featured their share of skyscrapers over the years. From The Big E to Mo Malone and from the Twin Towers to Yao Ming, Houston has always featured scintillating inside play. And like the city of Houston, the Rockets have a rich history but are also focused on the future. Perhaps with proper alignment of the stars, today's Rockets can launch themselves to more titles in the years ahead.

INDEX